Rockwell:
A Boy and His Dog

Loren Spiotta-DiMare

Illustrated by Cliff Miller

"Scotty, Mr. Rockwell called. He's ready to start a new painting and said to bring your plaid jacket, red scarf, and blue knit cap."

"Okay, Mom," Scotty Ingram replied. Since it was summer he ran up to the attic to dig through his winter clothes. He already knew to wear his blue jeans. Mr. Rockwell always liked them. Then he dashed through the streets of Stockbridge to reach the art studio on time.

The thin, gray-haired man sat on a wooden chair in front of his easel puffing on a favorite pipe. Wearing a suit and bow tie, Norman Rockwell, America's most famous artist, looked like a businessman except for his paint-splattered sneakers! Suddenly, the young boy bounded in.

4

"Hello, Scotty. How's my favorite model?" Rockwell asked in a deep, gravelly voice.

"Just fine, Sir," Scotty replied trying not to giggle. Such a burly voice coming from the skinny artist always sounded funny to Scotty. "What are we working on today?"

"Oh, you're sure to like these," Rockwell answered with a kind smile.

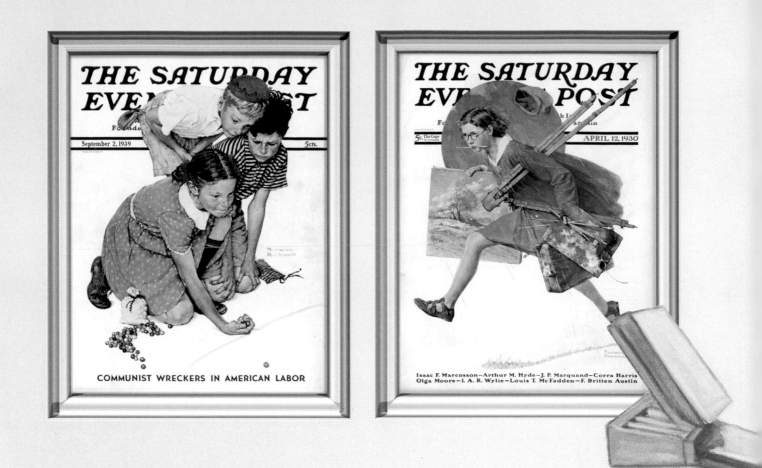

THE SATURDAY EVENING POST

September 2, 1939   5cts.

COMMUNIST WRECKERS IN AMERICAN LABOR

APRIL 12, 1930

Isaac F. Marcosson—Arthur M. Hyde—J. P. Marquand—Corra Harris
Olga Moore—I. A. R. Wylie—Louis T. McFadden—F. Britten Austin

"I'm creating four calendar paintings, one for each season," Rockwell explained. "I'm calling them *A Boy and His Dog*."

Scotty's eyes grew wide. "Can Uncle Fud, our Basset Hound, be the dog?" he asked quickly.

"Uncle Fud's a swell dog," Rockwell replied. "Reminds me of a dog I had long ago, but he doesn't have quite the look I'm after."

"What kind of dog are you looking for?" Scotty asked, trying to hide his disappointment.

"I'm not sure yet. But we'll find him. Don't you worry," Rockwell said. "Now let's set you up in the first pose."

There was a box in the middle of the studio stuffed with a pillow and covered by a sheet. "That's our dog for the moment," Rockwell explained. "Now Scotty, please scrunch down next to the box and place your hand on the pillow as if you were petting the dog. Oh, and hold this change purse in your left hand."

"Sure thing, Mr. Rockwell," Scotty replied.

"You're meeting the dog for the first time and are planning to buy him," Rockwell explained. "Try to look happy and serious at the same time. This is an important day for the boy in the painting."

After a while, Scotty began to wiggle. "Everything okay?" the artist asked.

"It's a little warm in here, Sir," Scotty explained.

"I thought you might be uncomfortable in those winter clothes," Rockwell replied. "Hold on just a while longer and then we'll go across the street and buy ourselves a couple of chocolate milk shakes."

The next time Scotty walked into the studio, Rockwell pointed to a stool and handed him a bottle of medicine and a spoon. "The dog's not feeling well in this painting," the artist explained. Scotty nodded and sat quietly on the stool. "You seem a little sad today, Scotty," Rockwell commented. "How's school going?"

"Not too well, Sir," Scotty replied with a sigh. "School is not my favorite subject."

Rockwell smiled, put down his paintbrush and walked over to Scotty. He placed his hand on the young model's shoulder. "You know Scotty, school wasn't my favorite subject either."

"It wasn't?" Scotty looked up in surprise.

"Nope," Rockwell replied. "And to make matters worse, I was pale, skinny, and funny-looking, so some of the other kids picked on me."

"They did?" Scotty asked, finding it hard to believe anyone would make fun of the famous artist.

"But I could draw and everyone seemed to like my drawings. So you see, things will get better."

As soon as he entered the studio to pose for the third painting, Scotty started talking. "I'm trying to find the right dog for you," the young model said to Rockwell. "John has an Irish Setter and Pete owns a Collie."

"A little too large," the artist responded. "I'm looking for a smaller dog, maybe a Beagle or Spaniel. But thanks for asking around." Scotty lay on a stack of pillows and placed his hand on the back of the pretend dog.

"Do you like being an artist, Mr. Rockwell?" he asked, suddenly gazing at all the paintings in the studio and a bag of fan mail on the floor. Rockwell was quiet for a while and then responded thoughtfully, "I think of myself as an illustrator because all my paintings tell a story. And yes, I like what I do very much.

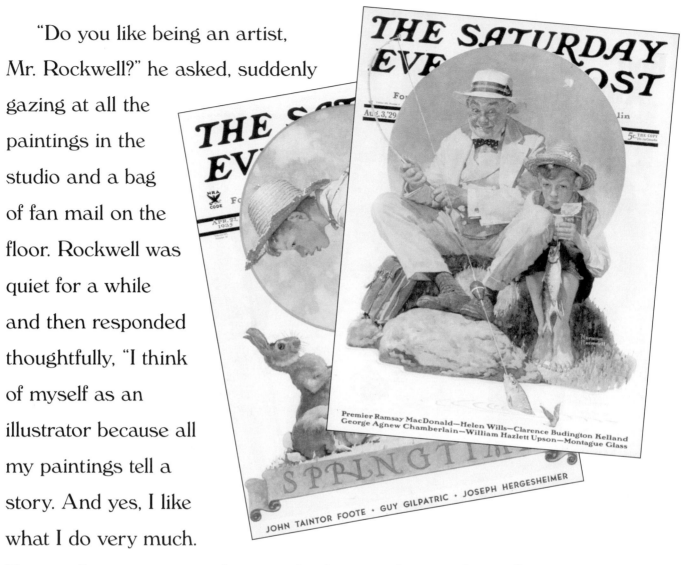

Especially painting regular people doing ordinary things."

"Everyone thinks you're a terrific artist!" Scotty replied. "Mom says there are lines of people at the newsstand just to see your *Saturday Evening Post* covers."

Rockwell smiled. He was always happy to hear compliments about his illustrations. To capture the simple pleasures of American life, he painted every day, even on birthdays and holidays, to be the very best he could be.

Later, while Scotty rode bikes through town with some of his buddies, Rockwell pedaled by in the opposite direction.

"That's my pal, Norman Rockwell," Scotty announced proudly.

"Oh, sure," his friend, Bobby said.

"Yes, he is!" Scotty insisted. "I pose for him all the time, and we have milk shakes together, and . . . ."

Just then Rockwell waved to the boys.

"Hi, Scotty, come join me."

Scotty waved back and turned his bike around.
His friends followed, and soon they
were all riding through town with
Norman Rockwell, the country's
most loved artist.

On his way home, Scotty noticed a small brown and white dog following Uncle Fud. He called to her but she hid her tail between her legs and ran off.

"Mom, did you see the dog hanging around with Uncle Fud?" Scotty asked as he ran into the house.

"No, I didn't Scotty," Mrs. Ingram replied. "Maybe she's a stray."

"I'll try to catch her," he said, grabbing some dog biscuits from the cabinet.

Scotty walked across the yard calling to the dog. "Here girl, here girl. Don't be afraid." But she had disappeared. He left the biscuits on a plate near the back porch.

After school the next day, Scotty brought a dish of food outside. Soon he saw a black nose peeking out from under the porch. The lost dog wiggled all the way out and gobbled up the food.

Scotty talked to her quietly. "Easy, girl. That's a good girl," he said gently. The little Beagle wagged her tail and followed him into the house to greet Uncle Fud.

"Looks like we have a new friend," Mrs. Ingram laughed. "I better phone the dog pound to see if her owners are looking for her." After she made the call, Mrs. Ingram turned to Scotty and said, "No one has reported a missing Beagle. I guess the next thing to do is run a Lost Dog ad in the local newspaper just to be sure."

"Okay, Mom, but I'm taking her to Mr. Rockwell's studio tomorrow," Scotty replied. "He's been looking for a Beagle for his calendar paintings."

LOST AND FOUND

Found female beagle in Stockbridge

Scotty couldn't wait to show the little stray to Mr. Rockwell. When he arrived at the studio, the artist was puffing on his pipe and already working. The boy and dog burst into the room.

"Well, well, what have we here?" Mr. Rockwell asked Scotty.

"I found her. She's a Beagle," Scotty replied excitedly.

"She certainly is," Rockwell responded. Very quietly the dog sniffed Rockwell's pants, wagged her tail, then hopped into a basket in the corner of the room. Rockwell and Scotty both laughed.

"Look at that," Rockwell said. "She's already posing."

"You said you were thinking of a Beagle or a Spaniel for the calendar paintings. So I had to bring her over," Scotty explained and shared the story of how he caught the dog.

"She sure is a lucky lady to find you," Rockwell said. "Shall we call her Lucky Lady?"

"That's a great name," Scotty replied. "Mom is trying to find her owners but I thought she could stay with you for a while."

"Sure, she can. I miss having a dog and she seems to like it here," Rockwell said.

The artist spent hours painting Lucky Lady. Scotty stopped by to visit now and then.

"Mr. Rockwell," he said one afternoon. "No one has called to ask about Lady."

"I think I'll keep her then," Rockwell said. "She's a sweet dog and seems to like me."

Scotty was pleased to hear the news and smiled as he looked over the paintings of himself and Lucky Lady. "Will we be starting on the last painting soon?" he asked.

"In a few more weeks," Rockwell replied. "I've finally decided what the painting should be about."

"Will you tell me?" Scotty asked.

"You'll see. It's a surprise. I'll call you when I'm ready," Rockwell responded.

When Scotty received the call to pose for the fourth painting, he rushed to the studio. As he opened the door he heard some funny yipping and yapping sounds. Then he saw Lucky Lady surrounded by five puppies.

"How do you like my surprise?" Rockwell asked as Scotty dashed over and knelt down to play with the pups.

"It's the best, Sir," he answered with a wide smile.

"Don't move," Rockwell said pulling out his paintbrush. "That smile is just what I'm looking for."

28